WILD

HARMONY

URBAN GARDENS BY BART & PIETER

Green & Bold
p 6

Selected Projects
p 16

Bowling
p 18

MVN
p 60

IPKW
p 68

AMS
p 78

PSLab
p 84

PAC
p 118

Burg
p 124

Bird's Nest
p 130

Ateliers van Lissum
p 140

Klingelbeek
p 176

Snapshots
p 192

Forever Vacation
p 194

CW Shop
p 196

Twiggy
p 206

La Chumbera
p 208

Our Garden
p 213

Our Studio
p 216

Celine
p 28

Hessen
p 40

Printery
p 48

NH
p 54

Paris / Texas
p 90

Loft 4C
p 98

Dam
p 106

Anyplace
p 114

Panorama
p 148

Pantheon
p 156

River Scheldt
p 162

Forge
p 168

Tar Factory
p 198

Veranda
p 200

Royal
p 202

Tanker
p 204

Plant List
p 220

Green & Bold: The Journey of Bart & Pieter

What is a landscape designer? To be fair, we don't remember exactly when we started referring to ourselves as such because we rolled into landscaping so gradually almost thirty years ago. Looking back at the projects that we have completed over the years, we — and our clients with us — have observed an evolution in our work and our interpretation of our role as landscape designers. An evolution that feels completely natural due to the experience and (plant) knowledge we gained and the influence of our personality on the creative process. An evolution that is also inevitable in view of the changing conditions in which our and all gardens must grow and flourish — yes, climate change is real. Obviously, we have taken this on board in everything we do. In fact, it has even become a decisive factor in the choices we make because we consider it our responsibility to provide answers to the challenges posed by climate.

The evolution in our work and how we can continue to build time and again on the knowledge and experience we gained over time is why we thought it would be inspiring and instructive (and also fun) to reflect on and look back at the gardens that we have designed and created over the past few years. It's the reason why we wanted to write this book. A lot of discussion went into it as we considered all our projects, whittling them down to a 'best of' of the past decade. We have chosen to limit ourselves to the last ten years for two reasons: firstly because we have already published books (in 2004 and 2011) with overviews of our projects. Secondly, because the evolution we mentioned has been much more apparent in the past ten years. Obviously, our older projects are also important, and the early years of our careers proved an indispensable learning experience that we look back on with fondness. But over the past decade, we have found our own signature style. A recognisable style that clients find appealing and the reason why they want to work with us. Some may find it rebellious. We think it is natural in every sense of the word.

Over the past decade, the seeds of our style and approach have blossomed.

This book is a spontaneous record of this process and what it has inspired to date. The projects we selected are examples of what you can do in an (urban) garden or on a (rooftop) terrace. Because so much is possible with so little effort and maintenance on a limited budget. With the right choices, you can create gardens on just a few square metres of unpaved soil that immediately and naturally develop into fully-fledged ecosystems. One well-placed and well-chosen tree can provide shade, coolness and a calming view for all your neighbours. The fact that we were able to acquire the knowledge to choose the most suitable trees, plants and substrates for such projects over the years feels like a privilege and is perhaps one of our most satisfying achievements.

The photos on the following pages show how each of our gardens has specific features. You will see gravel in many of the pictures. We like to use this substrate for several reasons, mainly ecological ones. We avoid tropical hardwood or containers unless they are made from reclaimed materials. Substrate, flagstones and even ordinary paving stones are also making a comeback in our gardens. Our guiding principle is the simpler, the better. This applies to the materials we use and often also to our landscape designs. They are always plant-based, starting from the uniqueness of each plant to create a painting, with different scenes, depth and colour. We very consciously choose to let the plants tell the story, allowing the garden to live and flourish in all its wild and untamed beauty.

On the following pages, you will get an idea of what we find important as landscape architects. For us, this book cements what we have increasingly come to regard as our mission, namely to create added value beyond the individual garden. It is our hope that we can change people's perspective of greenery and nature through our work. Our aim is to show them that gardens can be a source of beauty, health and quality of life rather than something that needs to be contained or controlled. The freer the rein we give nature, the more nature can give us, including clean air and moments of quiet wonder, as well as inspiration and perhaps even chances of survival. Building on this philosophy, we have tried to incorporate specific core values into each of our landscape designs over the past decade. These key concepts characterise both us and our work, and we hope that they will inspire people to loosen the reins and make space for nature.

SUSTAINABLE

Gardens are not flower arrangements. They are not temporary creations that you can enjoy for a few weeks, after which you discard them. Gardens are for eternity, or at least for as long as possible. Obviously, we also want to create beauty and a strong visual impact with our designs. Increasingly, however, our emphasis is on sustainability. We choose perennials rather than annuals, because they come back every year. The mixed borders we design don't need

to be replanted time and again because the plants multiply every year. Although plant diversity may decrease over time, the borders will become fuller and more abundant, allowing you in time to start selecting.

Where possible, we use natural materials that you can recover. If and when we use paving, we lay it on a substrate so it can be reused. We try to avoid paving if at all possible, which can be especially challenging in rooftop gardens, which have accounted for a large part of our portfolio in recent years. Instead, we prefer substrate (a volcanic soil with a gravel structure). Its structure doesn't change. After ten, fifteen or even twenty years, it is still as permeable as ever. Sustainability is also the reason why we now tend to go for no-lawn designs. Lawns need a lot of water and attract fewer insects, whereas our aim nowadays is to create as much biodiversity as possible with our designs. This partly explains why we like gravel so much: while it may not seem ecological, many plants thrive in it.

DROUGHT & HEAT RESISTANT

Drought resistance is crucial if you want to reconcile sustainability with climate change, dictating our choice of plants: Mediterranean plants such as rosemary and lavender are increasingly preferred to the detriment of our traditional native species that are used to a lot of rain. Our planting scheme has evolved considerably if you look at our older designs, thanks in part to our own garden in Menorca, where we can freely test our ideas for dry, sunny gardens.

We create gardens that do not need too much water where possible, but our rooftop gardens always rely on irrigation. We continue to look for ways to reconcile this need with sustainability. When designing a rooftop garden for a new construction project, we prefer to be involved in the architectural process as early as possible so we can ask the designers to provide for adequate rain harvesting. These days, 5,000 litres is the standard, but this isn't sufficient for a roof garden. In practice, harvesting more water means having to give up something, like parking spaces, for example, which means less revenue for the property developer. However, we see it as our moral duty to strive for rainwater harvesting and gardens that require as little extra water as possible and to look for creative solutions to this quandary.

The same applies to shade. For a recent project, we planted a large number of fifty-year-old pines, birches, oaks and holly around a building in a sustainable business park in the Dutch Veluwe region. The idea is that it will grow into a wild forest with other trees in between, becoming a source of clean air, biodiversity and cooling. Hopefully, it will inspire the owners of the other buildings to create a slice of nature and let it grow wild instead of opting for a rigid park design.

No garden can survive without shade. Fortunately, these days, there are many more possibilities than you might think. Small interventions, such as one well-placed tree with the right crown or a climbing plant against the façade, make all the difference. A deciduous shade tree such as an espaliered lime tree or a plane tree next to your bedroom window blocks the sun in summer and lets the light through in winter: a much more efficient, cheaper and infinitely more sustainable option than an awning with a remote control and a wind meter.

We find the challenges of urban and rooftop gardening both fascinating and inspiring.

TAILORED TO THE ENVIRONMENT

When we design a garden, we always start from the environment and the surroundings. We adapt our design to the reality we encounter, not the other way around. How is the garden oriented, is it overlooked by neighbours, is there shade, what does the view look like, are noise and wind a problem? The garden's situation determines its design. A garden with lots of sunshine requires a Mediterranean planting or typical coastal planting scheme with silver-leaved plants that don't need too much water. Add a simple pergola into this mix, and the result is a tremendously atmospheric ensemble.

Urban and rooftop gardens rarely provide ideal growing conditions for many plants or for grass, but we find the challenges we encounter in this setting both fascinating and inspiring. It is in self-limitation that the master first reveals himself: every problem is an opportunity to invent new possibilities. In roof gardens, the maximum weight that the roof can bear is our biggest foe, putting many dreams out of reach. At the same time, it also forces you to be creative and think about what is possible: a different, lighter substrate mixture with clay granules, potting soil or peat and plants and grasses that don't root as deep. Wind is also a determining factor on roofs. These days, we know which plants work in a given situation, and so we often end up with a similar list in similar conditions. The conditions on a windy

and sunny rooftop terrace are almost the same as on the coast, so the plants and trees you find in the dunes also thrive on rooftops. By adapting our design maximally to the environment, we give greenery the best chance to survive among all the concrete.

ON THE GROUND

Everything we know, everything we have learnt in recent years, we owe to our experience on the ground. Instead of designing gardens at our desks, we head out into the field. We know that wisteria does very well on a windy roof terrace because we observed this ourselves, in all the years we have been creating gardens. We have also seen many other plants that failed to thrive in this setting. We know that rhododendrons are the best choice for acidic soils with a high pH because once the garden has been laid out, we keep in touch with the client and go on site ourselves to see which plants flourish where.

To us, creating gardens involves so much more than garden design. We still build our gardens ourselves, with a team that has been hand-picked specifically for the project. The balance between the creative and physical aspects of our job is something we are not prepared to let go of for the time being. We like to keep an overview, and Pieter oversees every step of the process behind the scenes, right down to the logistical planning of the day of execution. Providing road signage or arranging for the giant crane to be on site at the right time to lift mature trees over houses: building a garden is a very complex process, and for that reason, we have chosen to limit the number of projects we take on each year.

We are always there when the spade finally goes into the ground because we want the option to determine on the spot, right there and then, exactly where the new tree should be planted or how the plants should be arranged. We rarely make detailed plans. Instead we prefer sketches, so we can fill the border intuitively on the day itself and make adjustments according to circumstances.

INTUITIVE & ORGANIC

Increasingly our approach is intuitive, at times impulsive even. A design is never created behind the computer but in Bart's head during his initial site visit together with the client. There has to be a click. This first meeting on site usually becomes a brainstorming session, during which Bart and the clients get to know each other. He listens to their wishes while taking in the surroundings, identifying constraints and visualising what is possible. After this first intense discussion, Bart usually goes home with a clear outline already sketched in his head.

When Bart is on site and envisages what the garden might look like, he is filled with enthusiasm. As you watch him work, it feels as if he is dancing with the plants or waving imaginary colours and effects, like an artist working on a composition. Creativity and spontaneity play an increasingly important part in what we do. We are not afraid of letting our choices be guided by our inspiration in the moment, triggered by the environment, and fuelled by experiences and impressions.

 Our intuitive way of working also explains why our gardens are so personal. It is a luxury to be able to work with clients who know what we stand for because we have been in the business of creating gardens for so long. It is vital that there is a match, ensuring the client trusts our intuition because our designs are usually not very detailed. Sometimes, Bart decides on the spur of the moment which plants will go where just before they go into the ground. At the same time, we must also trust our clients because once a garden has been laid out, our chapter draws to a close. That is where the story really begins and we are always very curious about how it will continue. People who have a more relaxed approach to life tend to give their gardens more free rein and invest less time in maintenance. Clients who prefer sleek lines, no clutter, and organisation tend to keep a tighter rein. When we build a garden, we deliberately make the space for it so it can develop organically. We love seeing how a garden mirrors the client's personality.

Creativity and spontaneity play an increasingly important part in what we do.

Taman Bebek, Made Wijaya

A WINDOW TO THE WORLD

For Bart, while the experience in the garden is important, the view of the garden as experienced from the house is equally important. The circulation in the garden, the vistas, what you see when you look out of each window … The greenery outside also greatly influences life inside the house. You can camouflage or accentuate things; you can even add an entirely new dimension to a home. We prefer to create a wilder garden to offset sleek and minimalist interiors or even an uncontrolled forest that flows with the seasons. The view of such a rebellious, organic slice of greenery creates an enriching contrast.

A garden then is like a painting, and increasingly, we think that our work as landscape designers is very similar to that of a painter. Obviously, technical knowledge is of the greatest importance, but we should not be afraid of letting our gut instincts guide us. Because our designs are so intuitive, we find it important to feed our imagination. Something we mainly do by travelling far and wide. The garden of the house of Sri Lankan architect Geoffrey Bawa in Lunuganga made a huge impression on us, as did the roof gardens he designed for the Heritance Kandalama Hotel and the gardens of Taman Bebek, Made Wijaya's country house in Bali. The unique interaction between architecture and the environment in Bawa's work continues to serve as an inexhaustible source of inspiration, both in the choice of materials (the combination of gravel and rough stones) and in the myriad of ways to create perspectives and levels (Lunuganga's stairways are incredible). We also find the shade garden in Barcelona's Parc de la Ciutadella inspiring. We keep returning to it, gaining new insights and ideas. The same goes for Hanbury, a beautiful Mediterranean garden in Ventimiglia, and Le Jardin Plume in Picardy, with its unusual borders of grasses and flowers. Our visits to the botanical garden in Puerto de la Cruz in Tenerife and the work of César Manrique in Lanzarote led us to regularly use volcanic substrate as paving ourselves.

Puerto de la Cruz, botanical garden

Mexico City, Luis Barragán

Kandalama Hotel, Geoffrey Bawa

come poking around. (Few people are aware of how many birds you can spot in a small rooftop garden. They love these gardens because there are no cats.)

With our work and with this book, we want to show what is possible if you give nature a chance and let it run wild. In the city especially, where every little patch of unpaved land with planting is a small victory over concrete, which reigns supreme. We hope that the projects in this book will inspire readers to think differently about greenery and that we will all make more space for trees in the city to enjoy greater cooling, shade and diversity.

We want to show what is possible if you give nature a chance and let it run wild.

NATURAL SIMPLICITY

It is an interesting contrast: the more we have seen and lived, the more inspiring places and gardens we have visited, the more expansive our mental library and the richer our imagination, the greater our penchant for simplicity. You can see a clear trend: our designs have become simpler over the years, more plant-based without too many structures, and with one material where possible. While this is our philosophy — we want to create calming views for people and make our gardens as sustainable as possible — it is also practical and cheaper. The more techniques, the more people you need, which slows down the process and raises the price. We prefer to invest in plants rather than structures, a hedge rather than a balustrade.

The story of the gardens we create is told by the plants in them. We see ourselves as creators of space in which nature can take its course. You need to stop cutting the grass, pruning and curbing and give nature freedom and trust. Only then will you see a garden really come alive and, in our opinion, see it really come into its own. Plant a tree, two shrubs and some flowers, and after just a few hours, you'll already see bumblebees hovering and blackbirds

SELECTED PROJECTS

BOWLING

Patio garden of an advertising agency, 65 m²
Evergreen, tropical ambience
Outdoor meeting and lunch area

The round openings in the ceiling of this former car service centre inspired us to create an exotic patio. The garden gives out onto an office space with large windows, meaning the workers look out onto the garden year-round. That is why the garden had to be evergreen. To create visual appeal in summer and winter, we used lots of evergreen plants with a tropical feel that can thrive in our European climate.

The existing concrete floor was excavated to a depth of 40 centimetres and topped up with roof garden substrate. We laid gravel grids on the substrate for stability and created seating areas so the garden could also be used for lunch and meetings, becoming an additional (outdoor) space. The centrally planted silk tree (*Albizia julibrissin*) connects the courtyard garden with the outside world and will provide transparent shade over time. This is the first project where we went all the way with substrate as a paving material: sustainable, fertile, and very user-friendly.

Plan

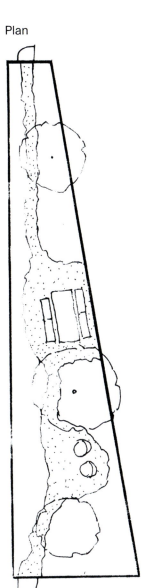

Before

CELINE

Garden in two parts, 54 m² & 310 m²
Lush enclosed oasis
Central holm oak for privacy

The architect of this project was clearly influenced by Bo Bardi's Brazil and Barragàn's Mexico, as evidenced by the home's colourful interior. This style inspired us to create a Mediterranean and subtle tropical planting plan. The project revolves around a beautiful mature tree that we planted in the centre of the garden: a *Quercus ilex* or holm oak, that looks similar to an old apple tree. Together with the client, we settled on a beautiful evergreen tree that provides shade and maximum privacy, which is essential in this enclosed garden as it is overlooked by several houses and a block of flats. Initially, the intention was not to plant such a large evergreen tree, but it was love at first sight for the client at the nursery.

We added a tall rhododendron with fuchsia flowers, tree ferns and cypress trees to create a lush, green oasis. We managed to create some sense of privacy between the winter living area (conservatory) and the neighbours on the left with a cluster of evergreen yews and *Carpinus betulus*. The plants in the central borders are very diverse, offering lots of variety in terms of shape, scent and colour throughout the year. We camouflaged the walls with various climbers, including evergreen Tuscan jasmine (*Trachelospermum jasminoides*) and Algerian ivy (*Hedera 'Gloire de Marengo'*), combined with deciduous species such as wisteria (*Wisteria sinensis*), *Clematis 'Étoile de Hollande'* and Boston ivy (*Parthenocissus t. veitchii*). We chose castle gravel for the paving because it is a nice match with the terracotta tiles of the two winter gardens.

Plan

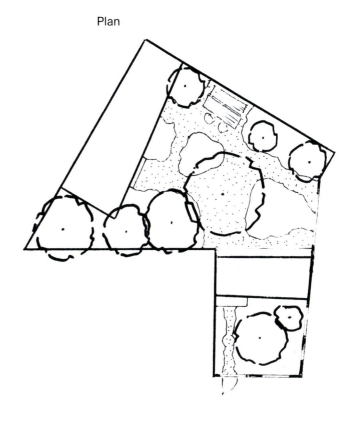

During

39

HESSEN

Roof garden, 196 m²
A lawn for a real garden feel
Pergola with wisteria

We wanted to create the illusion of an actual garden on this rooftop with a spectacular view of the city's most iconic building. The outdoor space is located above an industrial loft and can be accessed from a rooftop pavilion. We chose to add a lawn to make it feel more like a garden and provide a place to play for the client's dog. The skylights were concealed from view where possible, with a mix of perennials and grasses.

There is lots of sunshine to be had here, like on all roofs. However, it also means that you cannot sit in the garden if there are no shaded areas. At the client's request, we therefore built a large steel pergola overgrown with wisteria (*Wisteria sinensis*) to provide shade so the client could eat outside. False holly (*Osmanthus burkwoodii*) hedging serves as a balustrade. Bamboo sticks were woven into the hedge for added safety to ensure that even the dog would never be able to make it through the hedge.

Plan

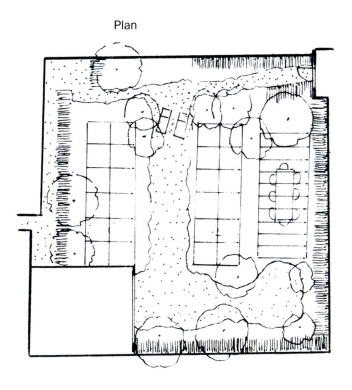

Before

PRINTERY

City garden, 40 m²
Central planting for depth
Deciduous trees for both shade and light

  From a former print shop with no outdoor space to a family home with lots of light and a green view: this project focused on the relationship between the garden and architecture, between indoor and outdoor spaces. The transition between the house and garden is gradual, through a greenhouse or winter garden, which becomes an extension of the living area, especially in autumn and spring. To protect the greenhouse from the summer heat, we planted some elegant trees close to the glass: thorny locust (*Gleditsia triacanthos*) and juneberry (*Amelanchier lamarckii*). These provide shade in summer but let through the light in winter. The trees also reduce the reflection of the glass of the greenhouse into the garden — this was a major issue for the plants due to the south-facing orientation — and conceal the rear façades of the surrounding houses.

  The garden is not very large, which is why we opted for central planting. That way, you cannot tell right away where the garden ends when looking at it from the house, which creates the illusion of more depth. We created a castle gravel path around this plant island to facilitate movement and as a play area for the client's children. The architect had designed a concrete bench along the entire length of the back wall, to which we added greenery in the centre with *Fatsia japonica*. We chose Virginia creeper (*Parthenocissus quinquefolia*) as a climber for the walls: in summer, the green leaves have an insulating effect against the heat, turning a beautiful orange in early autumn and red later in the season.

NH

Hotel patio, 138 m²
(Sub)tropical atmosphere
Eye-catcher/garden view

Right in the station district, on the roof of a car park, imagining yourself in a tropical garden: that is the effect we had in mind. The patio is situated in the heart of an eight-storey hotel with about eighty rooms, all overlooking the garden. You can see the garden in the background from the lobby: a real eye-catcher the minute you enter the hotel. On sunny days, the hotel bar spills out onto the terrace. We were inspired by the hotel's cosmopolitan atmosphere, a place where people from all over the world come and go. We chose tropical-looking plants that briefly give you the illusion that you have landed in the tropics and evergreens where possible, so hotel guests always have a view of a lush garden in January and August alike. The hotel has left the garden virtually undisturbed since its construction, with excellent results: it requires very little maintenance, and the plants have grown nicely since then.

The black volcanic roof garden substrate matches the garden's tropical atmosphere, and the colour contrasts nicely with the greenery and the dark patio tiles. We used it as a substrate and for the footpath through the garden. Guests can thus enter the garden and walk from one terrace to the other, although it was primarily created for viewing purposes and as a calming feature in a busy city. To add some greenery to the stone and concrete surroundings, we created two similar gardens on the adjacent roofs.

Before

During

MVN

Two roof gardens, 75 m² & 48 m²
Lush greenery for privacy
Recovery of the original tiles

We transformed two paved roof terraces into green roof gardens in a prime location in Ghent, in the historic city centre. The parallel gardens flank a penthouse. The terrace at the rear was overlooked by a block of flats. We planted a green buffer for more privacy, which acts like an outdoor curtain, with pines, silverberry and sea buckthorn. The front terrace, meanwhile, has a nice view of the historic city centre. Instead of camouflaging it, this is a feature you want to accentuate. On either side, we created open spaces to eat or relax.

We wanted the terraces to become a green extension of the indoor space, highlighting the strong indoor-outdoor connection. Densely planted borders with lots of diversity and an emphasis on evergreens were therefore planted right up to the windows. Although we left some tiles in the garden to be used as seating areas and paths, we removed most of them, replacing them with roof garden substrate. We planted drought-loving and wind-resistant plants (yuccas, rosemary) and trees, including Scots pine (*Pinus sylvestris*) and stag's horn sumach (*Rhus typhina*); the latter is a reliable wind-resistant plant that fans out like a parasol and provides shade very quickly.

Plan

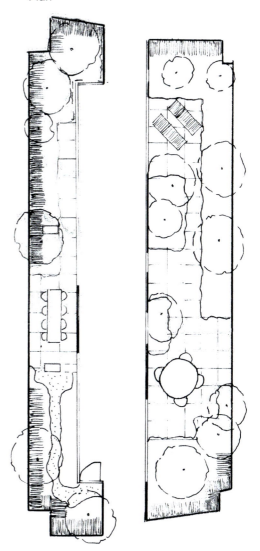

Before

IPKW

Roof garden corridor, 150 m²
Forest against the end wall, 300 m²
Courtyard forest main hall, 100 m²
Wild, brutalist atmosphere
Inspired by De Hoge Veluwe

Industriepark Kleefse Waard (IPKW) is the most sustainable business park in the Netherlands. The 90-hectare site near Arnhem is home to several sustainable energy-related companies. Here we planted a woodland area in the corridor, near the end wall and inside the main hall of Building KB. A former chemical plant, it was renovated and now houses an innovation lab, among others. Our starting premise was to ask ourselves what would grow here without any human intervention over one hundred years. The nearby De Hoge Veluwe nature reserve provided the answer: a mixture of birch, oak, and Scots pine with an undergrowth of ferns, grasses, and bluebells. We selected these native species for the outside corridor and for the forest against the end wall. As for the trees, we decided to plant larger trees to make it look like they grew there naturally many years ago. We wanted our planted forest to serve as a model for the other buildings on the site. Hopefully, this pioneering project will be the first of many green zones on the site, allowing nature to take its course and compensate for the concrete.

We also felt that the wild, natural atmosphere paired nicely with the brutalist look of the industrial buildings. Inside the hall, we also wanted to recreate a forest to soften the building's hard concrete architecture somewhat and, more importantly, create a focal point in this vast indoor space. Here we needed to choose trees that thrive in an indoor climate. We ended up settling on tropical black olive trees (*Bucida buceras*) in various forms. We added a mix of ferns and lilyturf for the undergrowth. Additional grow lights were installed to compensate for the lack of natural light in the garden.

AMS

Rooftop and patio garden, 500 m² & 200 m²
A meeting place for a management school
Plus two smaller viewing gardens

Two restored historic buildings and a new-build form the campus of this management school. A central foyer and a spacious multifunctional auditorium connect the new and the historic buildings, providing access to a courtyard garden and a rooftop garden. In the patio garden on the ground floor, we started by planting two large green trees to counterbalance the many surrounding buildings. We chose thorny locust (*Gleditsia triacanthos*): these trees grow quickly, and their foliage lets through a lot of light so that a lot can still grow underneath. Here we opted for a mix of perennials, with evergreen species such as Christmas rose (*Helleborus orientalis*) and Morrow's sedge (*Carex morrowii 'Mosten'*), as well as other flowering species such as *Azalea japonica* and *Geranium 'Rozanne'*. At the edges of the garden, we planted mind-your-own-business, which will eventually grow through the cracks between the cobblestones.

The rooftop garden on the first floor is accessible to everyone at all times and serves as a meeting place for employees, students and visitors. At the client's explicit request, we provided a number of breakout zones where people can work, meet or relax away from others. We planted various fruit trees and many flowering plants here to increase biodiversity. The garden has thus become the campus 'park' and a green lung in the heart of the city. We also created two smaller patios in the foyer as evergreen viewing gardens. Here we used *Fatsia japonica*, *Osmanthus burkwoodii*, soft shield fern (*Polystichum setiferum*) and hart's tongue fern (*Asplenium scolopendrium*), among others. The snowy mespilus (*Amelanchier lamarckii*) bear beautiful white blossoms in early spring and add wonderfully dramatic colour in autumn.

PSLAB

Winter garden, 45 m²
Mediterranean plants in pots
Work and lunch area

    This unheated winter garden is part of the office space/showroom of a company that designs luminaires. The designers' offices are in a former warehouse from the early 1900s, which was repurposed without sacrificing its industrial character. The structure is that of a simple open hall, with an impressive steel construction. Typically, warehouses are enclosed and dark; in this case, a conservatory was added at the rear on the first floor to subtly draw in natural light.

    We planted this winter garden with a mix of mainly evergreen Mediterranean plants: Japanese loquat, fig tree, paperplant, succulents and more. All the plants are in pots like in a real orangerie. We chose different formats and materials: fibre cement (Eternit), wood, and terracotta. The mix creates a fun and somewhat rougher effect. The garden space primarily acts as a view from the office, but there is also a table at which you can work or have lunch.

PARIS / TEXAS

Patio garden, 24 m²
Evergreen tropical ambience
Eye-catcher of a home/studio/art gallery

The patio garden is the heart of this project in every sense. The garden can be seen from all the windows of the house, which is why we designed it in such a way that it is beautiful year-round with an evergreen structure (*Phyllostachys vivax*, *Fatsia japonica*, *Eriobotrya japonica* and *Dicksonia antarctica*). We created a mound in the centre with *Leptinella squalida* and a combination of exotic-looking plants such as *Anigozanthos flavidus* and *Anemone pamina*.

Our intention was to create a lush, vibrant look and blend the beauty of the garden with the interior and vice versa. To blur the line between indoor and outdoor living and emphasise the connection between the different functions, the house's bright yellow-painted walls extend seamlessly into the garden. The same applies to the concrete paving combined with shale chips. The house has been fitted with floor-to-ceiling sliding doors. When they are open, the barrier between inside and outside disappears. The eye-catcher is the dramatic *Dracaena marginata* or Madagascar dragon tree growing out of the concrete floor in the kitchen. It was planted using a crane, after which the glass roof was installed above it.

LOFT 4C

Roof garden, 140 m²
Patio/garden view, 16 m²
Sun-loving and wind-resistant plants (roof)
Shade-loving and evergreen plants (patio)

We started from the pine trees that we were able to recover from the existing roof terrace for our plan for this wild roof garden. They stood in large tubs on and around an existing wooden terrace clad with white floorboards. Our brief was to create a garden with enough shade. A pergola, against which we planted wisteria (*Wisteria sinensis*), played a crucial part in this. The Scots pines (*Pinus sylvestris*) that were already there thrive in full sun and wind. Instead of planting them in pots, we decided to plant them directly into the substrate. That way, they got a new lease of life. We also chose plants such as silverberry (*Elaeagnus ebbingei*), tamarisk, *Genista lydia*, *Yucca gloriosa* and holm oak (*Quercus ilex*).

The colour palette is mainly defined by shades of grey-green, with colour accents from poppies (*Papaver orientale 'Allegro'*) and wallflowers (*Erysimum 'Bowles Mauve'*), among others. The castle gravel paths accentuate the greenery and colours but also make the garden more pleasant for the client's dog. The roof garden is connected to the loft with stairs from the patio. This garden room in the heart of the house connects the various living areas. Large windows let the light flood in, offering views from all sides of evergreens, including mind-your-own-business (*Soleirolia soleirolii*) between the stepping stones and Tuscan jasmine (*Trachelospermum jasminoides*) against the bannister.

Plan

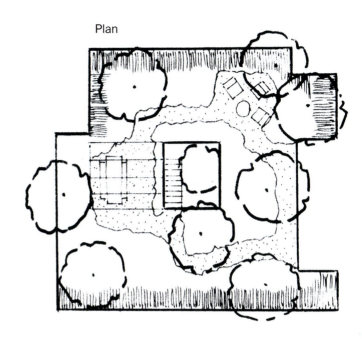

Before

DAM

City garden, 120 m²
Green zone between the house and the house behind it
Pavers and castle gravel

  This garden is located between two houses, which were completely renovated into a bright, contemporary single-family home. The garden links the front house and the annexe. Before the renovation, it was full of all kinds of outbuildings. Following the construction and demolition work, the ground level of the garden ended up being 40 centimetres lower than necessary. We shored it up with several big bags of vulcanised substrate that were lifted over the roof using a mobile construction crane. The crane also gave us an opportunity to plant two large trees as well. We chose a large evergreen cork oak (*Quercus suber*) for the gravel terrace. It provides a lovely evergreen view from the first and second floors of the front house, and also conceals some of the neighbours' somewhat untidy gardens from view. The other tree, a golden honey locust tree (*Gleditsia triacanthos 'Sunburst'*), was planted in front of the terrace of the annexe. This south-facing terrace needed some shade in summer.

  A paved path leads from the front house to the annexe at the rear. There is another terrace in the centre of this path, another spot to make the most of the sun at any time of the day in the garden. The planting is very diverse, with an emphasis on evergreens such as Mediterranean-looking shrubs, *Magnolia grandiflora*, Japanese loquat (*Eriobotrya japonica*), Chusan palm (*Trachycarpus fortunei*) and holm oak (*Quercus ilex*). Even more variety in shape and colour is provided by Mediterranean spurge (*Euphorbia characias 'Wulfenii'*), Mexican feather grass (*Stipa tenuissima*), *Crocosmia 'Lucifer'* and various herbs.

Plan

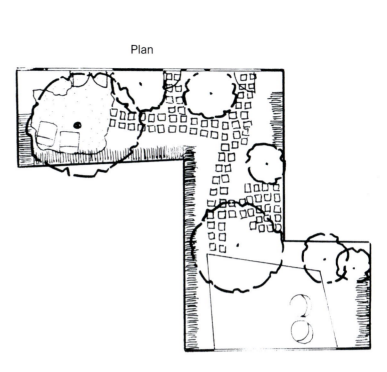

Before

ANYPLACE

Roof garden, 21 m²
Garden view
Natural Boston ivy roof

The primary function of this roof garden is to provide a nice green view for the residents. We also created two open spaces, however: one at the front left for breakfast in the morning sun and one at the rear right, against the wall, to enjoy the evening sun. The garden and loft are both south-facing. We therefore planted some stag's horn sumach to provide shade and coolness, both inside and outdoors. We also added an evergreen holm oak (*Quercus ilex*) in full view of the bedroom. Other evergreens include Tuscan jasmine (*Trachelospermum*), a beautiful climber that also smells good.

For added shade, we created a natural roof by stringing cables from wall to wall along which Boston ivy (*Parthenocissus quinquefolia*) grows; because it's a deciduous vine, the house feels brighter in winter. By pairing evergreen plants (such as *Viburnum tinus* and rosemary (*Rosmarinus officinalis*) with deciduous species, this garden offers the best of both worlds: always a green view, while still allowing you to see the seasons change.

PAC

City garden, 50 m²
Lots of evergreens
Mediterranean gravel garden

Initially, this walled city garden consisted of a concrete terrace behind the house and a lawn behind it. As is often the case in small city gardens, the lawn failed to thrive due to lack of light. The owners liked the terrace, however, because it was a sunny place to sit in summer, especially in the afternoon and evening. But they also wanted a shady spot to retreat to on hot days. So we created a second seating area in the middle of the garden, which we hid from view when looking from the house with a cleverly positioned central border. From inside the house, you now have a view of evergreen plants, with *Yucca gloriosa* for the most part.

We planted the rest of the garden with fairly large evergreens, more specifically, a mix of holly olive (*Osmanthus heterophyllus*) and glossy leaf paper plant (*Fatsia japonica*), among others. The planting makes it difficult to see exactly where the garden ends, which also makes the garden seem larger. There definitely is space to sit, but the garden also makes for a nice view from the house. The lush greenery provides a beautiful backdrop year-round, with castle gravel used for the paving. The gravel replaced the lawn and also became the terrace: we simply poured a layer on top of the existing concrete so nothing had to be broken up. As with most of our gardens, we opted for one type of paving. This uniformity also serves to make the garden seem larger.

Before

BURG

Roof garden, 65 m²
Nonchalant holiday atmosphere
Planting between gravel

This roof garden is located on top of an imposing townhouse in a prime location in the historic city centre. All it lacked, however, was an outdoor space. The roof garden solved this issue. Residents can have a meal or unwind there, and the garden also provides a view from the kitchen and living space. The travertine floor has been extended from the inside, blurring the boundary with the outdoor space. To accentuate this effect, we chose to pave the garden with gravel. In our opinion, gravel always creates a bit of a holiday atmosphere. This material also allowed us to merge the different areas in an informal way without having to strictly demarcate the path or space in front of the table.

While the planting seems casual, appearances can be deceiving. They are all strategically positioned to camouflage less attractive views and create more privacy. We used *Amelanchier lamarckii* and holm oak (*Quercus ilex*) for this. The choice of plants was determined by the location — they had to be suited to the conditions of a roof garden — but also by the ground cover: we wanted species that would pop out of the gravel. Naturally, we chose lots of evergreens, and at the request of the residents, we also added lots of fresh herbs.

BIRD'S NEST

Roof garden, 210 m²
A paradise for birds
Planting up to the façade

The owners of this duplex penthouse in the Brussels Periphery were looking for a compact home but also wanted to live in close proximity to nature, especially since they are avid bird watchers. Thanks to a wild and predominantly evergreen roof garden, this is perfectly possible. Better yet, indoor and outdoor spaces blend seamlessly here, an effect we have maximised by planting the garden right up to the façade and the large windows. That way, you enjoy natural shade inside, and when the floor-to-ceiling sliding doors are opened, you feel like you are outside inside. Here nature really starts on your doorstep, even though you are in a third-floor flat in a town centre.

We added paved areas throughout the garden, using the same volcanic roof garden substrate that we used for the plants. We created a spot so the owners can have their breakfast in the morning sun and another spot to lounge in the sun. Behind a technical unit, we also built a large terrace with a dining table and chairs. There, they are hidden from view to retain the green vista from the windows. The roof garden has been planted with trees and vigorously growing hedges. These camouflage the houses across the street and have become a safe haven for birds. The owners have even spotted crested tits and a kestrel. In some parts of the garden, we purposefully kept the planting low to highlight the great view of the church spire or the surrounding landscape. The colourful mix of woodland edges consists of silverberry (*Elaeagnus ebbingei*), sea buckthorn (*Hippophae rhamnoides*) and broom (*Cytisus scoparius*), combined with clusters of small trees: Scots pine (*Pinus sylvestris*), holm oak (*Quercus ilex*) and tamarisk. We also planted lots of herbs (rosemary, thyme, oregano) and Mediterranean-style plants and grasses.

Plan

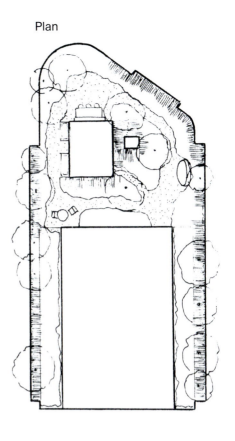

Before

ATELIERS VAN LISSUM

Roof garden, 110 m²
Patio garden, 10 m²
Rugged, natural effect
Woodland edges with native species

When you plant hedges and woodland edges, you attract insects and birds, and that is precisely what we intended to achieve with this project. The roof garden and patio are part of the house, while the communal inner area is a meeting place for residents and the creatives who work in one of the ten studios in the building. This building has a fascinating history: it predates the war and has previously been used as an industrial laundry, a diamond cutting and polishing factory, a karate club, and garages. Following a complete renovation, it was transformed into a hidden oasis where the city's hustle and traffic seem far away, with greenery playing a key role in the tranquillity.

The planting on the roof was deliberately chosen to ensure the garden largely obscures the surrounding rear façades. From the office, you have a view of the life that unfolds among the greenery. The roof garden is fascinating in every season, drawing nature into the heart of the city. Birds, flowers, insects and oxygen. Together with the client, we mainly chose native species such as woodland edges of hawthorn (*Crataegus monogyna*), beech (*Fagus sylvatica*) and hornbeam (*Carpinus betulus*), supplemented with lots of grasses (*Stipa brachytricha*) and many different perennials. Volcanic substrate and pavers provide a basic effect. This is how we like it: the plants do all the hard work, we enjoy seeing some grass and other pioneer plants grow between the pavers. The living area overlooks the patio behind the breezewall, another private slice of rugged nature. We also provided plenty of greenery at the entrance, with tall hedges of hornbeam, *Fatsia japonica*, ferns and evergreen grasses. The spot under the plane tree is a central meeting place. In time, the tree will provide enough shade for lunch or meetings.

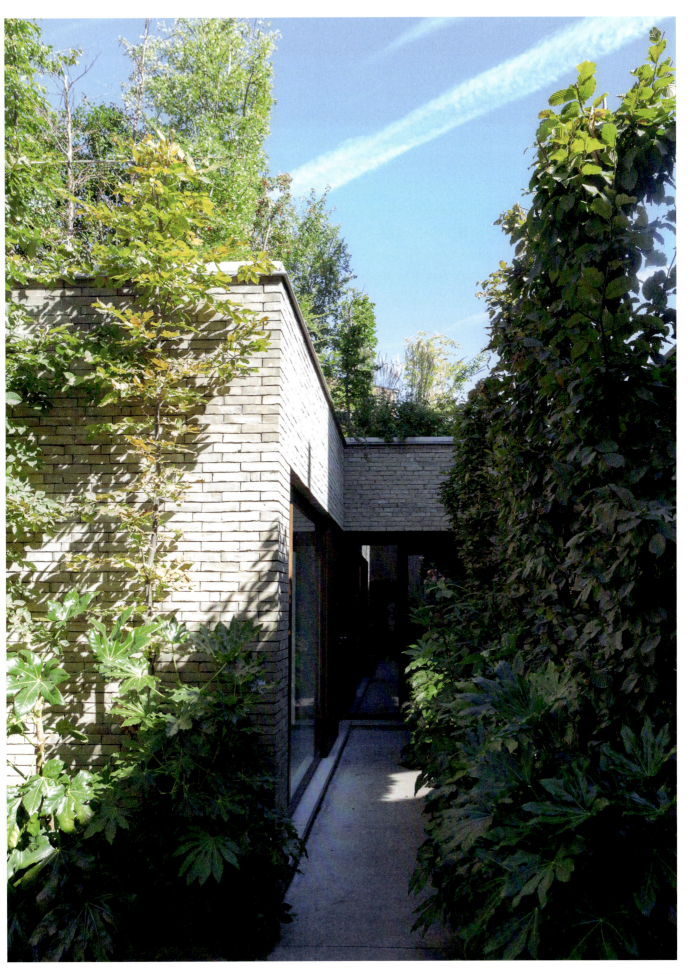

Before

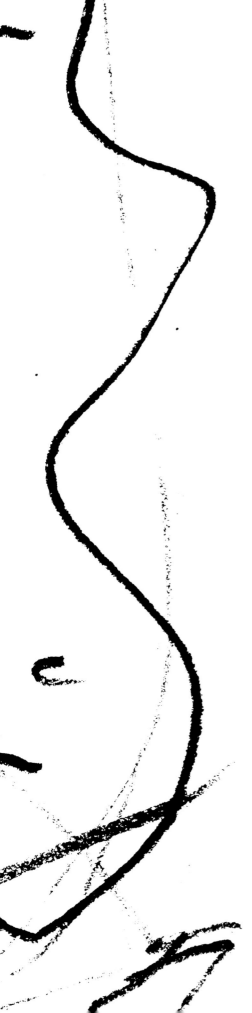

PANORAMA

Roof garden, 55 m²
View from the 21st floor
Low, evergreen planting

This roof garden is centrally located in a flat on the 21st floor: you look out onto it from just about every space in the living area. We therefore created a garden that stays green all year round, settling on low plants for the most part in order not to obscure the spectacular views of the port and city. The client specifically requested plants with little to no flowers. The roof's load-bearing weight provided an added challenge. We could not afford to take any risks in that area, all the more so because the original plans were no longer available.

To achieve as much of a garden feel as possible, the existing concrete tiles were removed, except under the seating area. Elsewhere, they were replaced by a 10-centimetre layer of roof garden substrate in which we planted evergreen species such as *Liriope muscari* and *Soleirolia soleirolii*, as well as shade plants such as ferns, which thrive on the otherwise sunny roof thanks to the canopy. We painted the concrete columns and roof structure black, wrapping them with climbers: *Trachelospermum jasminoides*, *Parthenocissus quinquefolia*, *Fatsia japonica* and *Rhus typhina*. Green always stands out beautifully against a black background, and this way, the garden also forms a harmonious unit with the dark colour palette of the interior design scheme. The large floor-to-ceiling windows provide a stellar view framed by greenery.

PANTHEON

City garden, 215 m²
Central pavilion with a vista
Shade garden in the back

This garden is located behind a stately mansion that dates from the 1920s. In the framework of a high-end renovation, we were asked to upgrade the garden and roof garden. We transformed the south-facing roof garden near the first-floor bedroom into a gravel garden with drought-resistant shrubs and perennials. In the downstairs garden, the pavilion is the real eye-catcher. It was there before we started. To us, it felt somewhat oriental, like a Thai temple. This inspired us to create a meditative space in and around it, but in such a way that there is more interaction with the greenery. We had the idea to remove the door at the front and open up the back of this little building. The result is a fun perspective, creating a view from the front to the very back of the garden.

The garden has two sections. The front, south-facing part is a sunny garden with flowering borders in different colours. To provide more shade on the rear façade of the house, we planted a relatively large golden honey locust tree (*Gleditsia triacanthos 'Sunburst'*) and an evergreen holly (*Ilex aquifolium*). Stepping stones in the lawn connect the terrace behind the house to a central terrace in the garden, which are both cast in polyconcrete. To soften the view, we lined the lawn with flowering perennials. The rear of the garden is a shade garden because of the many trees that were already there, including two Indian bean trees (*Catalpa bignonioides*). A woodchip path leads to the pavilion and beyond. Holly olive, yews, and hydrangeas do well here, with lilyturf (*Liriope muscari*), hart's tongue ferns (*Asplenium scolopendrium*) and sweet woodruff (*Galium odoratum*) for ground cover.

RIVER SCHELDT

Roof garden, 60 m²
Gravel garden with water feature
Renovation of an existing terrace

We transformed a roof terrace made of different materials with potted plants into a roof garden. At the residents' request, we sought to create a sense of tranquillity in the garden, with the panoramic view serving as the eye-catching feature of our design. In line with our philosophy, we opted for simple solutions where possible: fewer materials, more nature. We simplified the combination of wood and stone terraces on different levels by bringing everything to one level with castle gravel and much more planting.

The sleek yew hedge has been replaced with a dense, undulating hedge of silverberry (*Elaeagnus ebbingei*) and rugged coastal planting, which serves both as a balustrade and a windbreak. Around the pergola, we provided more space for climbers, including wisteria (*Wisteria sinensis*), a climber that is also very wind-resistant and provides plenty of shade. We retained the water feature with a filter zone of yellow iris (*Iris pseudacorus*) but transformed it into a plunge pool. The garden now looks wilder and more natural look, which is consistent with the gravel garden look we envisaged.

Before

FORGE

Roof garden, 100 m²
Vibrant mix of colours and textures
Limited load-bearing capacity

A former forge and coach house of an old chocolate factory was transformed into a beautiful single-family home. The owners were keen to create a roof garden in an urban environment to hide the surrounding buildings from view and create a greener vista from their patio and first-floor living space. At the same time, it also had to be a place where the family could spend time. We created two sitting areas among the greenery so you can choose where to sit depending on the season and the sun's position. The sitting areas are connected by a path made of the same volcanic substrate we used for the plants. That way, we created a 'walk' among the greenery.

The roof was not suited for the construction of a roof garden, meaning we had to take weight restrictions into account. We kept the substrate layer of the sitting areas and the connecting path as thin as possible so we could use a thicker layer for the planting and add larger plants. We looked for plants that do not root too deeply and ended up settling on drought-resistant varieties such as spreading rosemary (*Rosmarinus officinalis 'Prostratus'*), lavender cotton (*Santolina chamaecyparissus*), thyme and bearded iris (*Iris germanica*). The balustrade consists of a mixed hedge of silverberry, holm oak and sea buckthorn. Despite the roof's limited load-bearing capacity, we were able to create a wild garden with lots of colour and variation in any season that also camouflages the surrounding buildings.

Plan

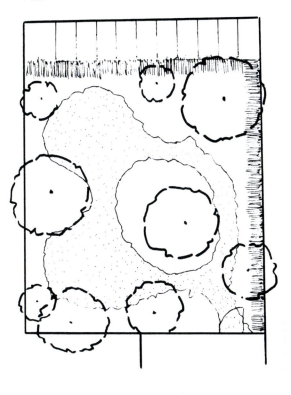

Before

KLINGELBEEK

Enclosed roof garden at the entrance, 110 m²
Rugged roof garden on the upper floor, 45 m²
Semitropical patio, 43 m²

The location of this project, a wooded estate on the banks of the Rhine, is unique, and the house itself is also very special. An annexe of a former monastery, it was converted into an experimental single-family home with bold materials and lots of colour. Our intention was to give a contemporary interpretation to the typical convent ambience with its enclosed gardens. This inspired us to create several green clusters. The monumental entrance door reveals a roof garden. The garden mainly provides a view from the kitchen and relaxation area, but thanks to stepping stones in different types of marble, it also serves as a passageway to the living area. We laid the stones in the substrate, between which we planted mind-your-own-business (*Soleirolia soleirolii*), which provides good ground cover and a lovely soft carpet of green. We also went for an eclectic mix of plants with lots of evergreens, such as holly olive (*Osmanthus heterophyllus*), *Euphorbia characias 'Wulfenii'* and *Eriobotrya japonica*, supplemented with Japanese maple and *Carex testacea*. Roses, wisteria and Boston ivy are led over the walls and cables.

There is a patio in the centre of the house. The star here is an impressive evergreen strawberry tree (*Arbutus unedo*) that bears red fruits that resemble strawberries in winter. The patio has to look good from every angle, which is why we added lush, diverse planting, including *Trachycarpus fortunei*, bamboo (*Fargesia robusta*) and *Mahonia media 'Charity'*. From the upper floor, you look down at what feels like a tropical valley. Near the bedroom, we created a rugged roof garden that withstands extreme conditions like the particularly strong winds and bright sunshine this garden has to contend with. The semi-paved area consists of a mix of coarse and fine gravel, with plantings including Scots pine (*Pinus sylvestris*), stag's horn sumach (*Rhus typhina*), *Yucca gloriosa* and grey plants such as rosemary, thyme and santolina or lavender cotton.

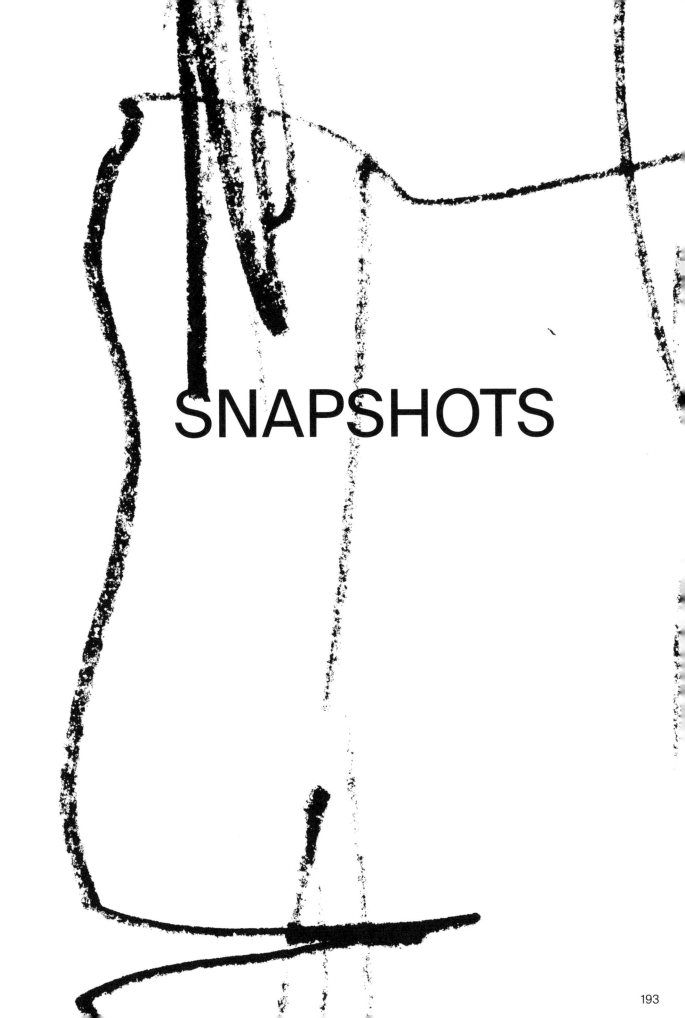

SNAPSHOTS

Forever Vacation — This 80-m² patio instantly brings a holiday feel to a former-chapel-turned-home.

CW Shop   A 12-m² lush, green living painting for Christian Wijnants's boutique.

Tar Factory — 180 m² rock and roll on the rooftop of a former factory.

Veranda   45 m² of nature as an extension of a restaurant.

Royal   A 160-m² garden for a true gardening enthusiast.

Tanker   As much greenery as possible for a roof garden (30 m²) with three skylights.

205

Twiggy   The green heart (44 m²) of a concept store.

La Chumbera Our 2,500-m² garden on Menorca for experimentation with drought-resistant varieties.

Our garden

A 3000-m² garden featuring a wildflower meadow in spring and mixed borders in summer.

Our studio   Our workspace in the city with its two courtyards.

Plant List

BOWLING

Trees & Shrubs
Albizia julibrissim
Amelanchier lamarckii
Eriobotrya japonica
Fargesia 'Jiu'
Fatsia japonica
Osmanthus aquifolium
Trachycarpus fortunei

Climbers
Actinidia deliciosa
Parthenocissus quincifolia
Trachelospermum jasminoides

Perennials & Grasses
Crocsomia 'Lucifer'
Kniphofia 'Alcazar'
Monarda squaw
Persicaria amplexicaulis
'Speciosa'
Polylstichum setiferum dahlem
Soleirolia soleirolii
Thalictrium delavayi
Veronica longifolia 'First match'

CELINE

Trees & Shrubs
Carpinus betulus
Cupressus sempervirens
Dicksonia antarctica
Eriobotrya japonica
Fatsia japonica
Ficus carica
Gleditsia triacanthos 'Sunburst'
Hydrangea macrophylla
Mahonia eurybracteata 'Soft
Caress'
Mahonia media 'Charity'
Rhododendron hybride
Trachycarpus fortunei
Quercus ilex

Climbers
Wisteria sinensis
Trachelospermum jasminoides

Perennials & Grasses
Crocosmia 'Lucifer'
Erysimum 'Bowles Mauve'
Euphorbia characias 'Wulfenii'
Foeniculum vulgare 'Giant

Bronze'
Geranium 'Rozanne'
Hemerocallis 'Aten'
Kniphofia 'Ice Queen'
Kniphofia 'Alcazar'
Monarda 'Cambridge Scarlet'
Persicaria amplexicaulis
'Speciosa'
Verbena bonariensis

HESSEN

Trees & Shrubs
Amelanchier lamarckii
Osmanthus burkwoodii
Rhus typhina
Viburnum tinus 'Eve Price'

Climbers
Wisteria sinensis

Perennials & Grasses
Carex howardii 'Phoenix Green'
Crocosmia 'Lucifer'
Nepeta faassenii 'Six Hills Giant'
Verbena bonariensis

PRINTERY

Trees & Shrubs
Amelanchier lamarckii
Fatsia japonica
Gleditsia triacanthos 'Sunburst'

Climbers
Parthenocissus tricuspidata
'Veitchii'

Perennials & Grasses
Carex morrowii 'Mosten'
Crocosmia 'Lucifer'
Erigeron karvinskianus
Euphorbia characias 'Wulfenii'
Geranium 'Rozanne'
Helleborus orientalis
Salvia nemorosa 'Ostfriesland'
Sanguisorba menziesii

NH

Trees & Shrubs
Amelanchier lamarckii
Camellia japonica
Carpinus betulus
Fargesia robusta 'Pingwu'
Fatsia japonica

Gleditsia triacanthos 'Sunburst'
Hydrangea aspera
Ilex aquifolium
Lonicera pileata
Magnolia grandiflora
Mahonia eurybracteata
'Soft Caress'
Nandina domestica
Osmanthus aquifolium
Trachycarpus fortunei

Perennials & Grasses
Asplenium scolopendrium
Carex morrowii 'Mosten'
Helleborus orientalis
Muehlenbeckia axillaris
Persicaria amplexicaulis
'Speciosa'
Persicaria bistorta
Soleirolia soleirolii
Zantedeschia aethiopica

MVN

Trees & Shrubs
Elaeagnus ebbingei
Hippophae rhamnoides
Pinus sylvestris
Rhus typhina
Tamarix ramosissima 'Pink
Cascade'
Yucca gloriosa

Climbers
Parthenocissus tricuspidata
'Veitchii'
Trachelospermum jasminoides
Wisteria sinensis

Perennials & Grasses
Agastache 'Blue Fortune'
Carex flacca 'Blue Zinger'
Centranthus ruber
Erysimum 'Bowles Mauve'
Euphorbia characias 'Wulfenii'
Gaura lindheimeri
Kniphofia 'Alcazar'
Lavandula angustifolia 'Hidcote'
Stachys byzantina
Thymus vulgaris

IPKW

Trees & Shrubs
Betula pendula
Bucida buceras
Cytisus scoparius

Ilex aquifolium
Osmanthus heterophyllus
Pinus sylvestris
Quercus robur

Perennials & Grasses
Carex pendula
Carex sylvatica
Dryopteris filix-mas
Molinia caerulea 'Heidebraut'

AMS LARGE PATIO

Trees & Shrubs
Gleditsia triacanthos 'Sunburst'

Perennials & Grasses
Carex morrowii 'Mosten'
Geranium 'Rozanne'
Soleirolia soleirolii

AMS SMALL PATIOS

Trees & Shrubs
Amelanchier lamarckii
Fatsia japonica
Mahonia eurybracteata
Osmanthus burkwoodii

Perennials & Grasses
Asplenium scolopendrium
Carex morrowii 'Mosten'
Helleborus orientalis
Polystichum setiferum
Soleirolia soleirolii

AMS LARGE ROOF GARDEN

Trees & Shrubs
Crataegus monogyna
Fagus sylvatica
Ligustrum vulgare
Malus domestica 'Elstar'
Osmanthus heterophyllus

Perennials & Grasses
Calamagrostis acutiflora
Carex oshimensis 'JS
Greenwell'
Crocosmia 'Lucifer'
Echinacea purpurea 'Pica Bella'
Euphorbia amygdaloides
'Robbiae'
Geranium 'Rozanne'
Helenium 'Moerheim Beauty'
Helleborus orientalis

Hemerocallis 'Sammy Russell'
Lavandula angustifolia 'Hidcote'
Monarda 'Squaw'
Nepeta faassenii 'Six Hills Giant'
Phlox amplifolia
Rudbeckia fulgida 'Goldsturm'
Salvia nemorosa 'Ostfriesland'
Verbena bonariensis

PSLAB

Trees & Shrubs
Chamaerops humilis
Citrus medica
Eriobotrya japonica
Fatsia japonica
Ficus carica
Magnolia grandiflora
Strelitzia reginae

Climbers
Monstera deliciosa
Vitis

Perennials & Grasses
Cyperus alternifolius
Aspidistra elatior

PARIS / TEXAS

Trees & Shrubs
Albizia julibrissim
Dicksonia antartica
Dracaena reflexa 'Angustifolia'
Eriobotrya japonica
Fatsia japonica
Phyllostachys vivax

Perennials & Grasses
Anemone hybrida 'Pamina'
Anigozanthos flavidus
Geranium 'Rozanne'
Heuchera micrantha 'Palace Purple'
Leptinella squalida

LOFT 4C ROOF GARDEN

Trees & Shrubs
Elaeagnus ebbingei
Genista lydia
Pinus mugo 'Mugo'
Pinus sylvestris
Quercus ilex
Rhus typhina
Tamarix ramosissima 'Pink Cascade'
Yucca gloriosa

Climbers
Wisteria sinensis

Perennials & Grasses
Erigeron karvinskianus
Erysimum 'Bowles Mauve'
Euphorbia characias 'Wulfenii'
Helleborus orientalis
Lychnis coronaria
Nepeta faassenii 'Walker's Low'
Papaver orientale 'Allegro'
Santolina chamaecyparissus
Stachys byzantina

LOFT 4C PATIO

Trees & Shrubs
Fatsia japonica
Mahonia eurybracteata 'Soft Caress'
Osmanthus burkwoodii
Rhus typhina

Climbers
Trachelospermum jasminoides

Perennials & Grasses
Asplenium scolopendrium
Carex oshimensis 'JS Greenwell'
Helleborus orientalis
Polystichum braunii
Soleirolia soleirolii

DAM

Trees & Shrubs
Elaeagnus ebbingei
Eriobotrya japonica
Eucalyptus gunnii
Fatsia japonica
Gleditsia triacanthos 'Sunburst'
Magnolia grandiflora
Quercus ilex
Quercus suber
Trachycarpus fortunei

Perennials & Grasses
Crocosmia 'Lucifer'
Erigeron karvinskianus
Euphorbia characias 'Wulfenii'
Geranium 'Rozanne'
Nepeta faassenii
Santolina chamaecyparissus

Soleirolia soleirolii
Stipa tenuissima

ANYPLACE

Trees & Shrubs
Quercus ilex
Rhus typhina
Viburnum tinus 'Eve Price'

Climbers
Parthenocissus quinquefolia
Trachelospermum jasminoides

Perennials & Grasses
Campanula poscharskyana 'Stella'
Carex testacea
Echinacea purpurea 'Pica Bella'
Hemerocallis 'Aten'
Rosmarinus officinalis
Thymus vulgaris
Verbena bonariensis

PAC

Trees & Shrubs
Acer palmatum
Ficus carica
Mahonia eurybracteata 'Soft Caress'
Nandina domestica
Osmanthus heterophyllus
Yucca gloriosa

Climbers
Parthenocissus tricuspidata 'Veitchii'
Wisteria sinensis

Perennials & Grasses
Crocosmia 'Lucifer'
Euphorbia characias 'Wulfenii'
Geranium 'Rozanne'
Helleborus orientalis
Papaver orientale 'Victoria Louise'

BURG

Trees & Shrubs
Amelanchier lamarckii
Camellia japonica
Fatsia japonica
Hydrangea macrophylla 'Twist-n-Shout'

Phyllostachys vivax
Quercus ilex
Viburnum bodnantense 'Dawn'
Viburnum tinus 'Eve Price'

Perennials & Grasses
Campanula lactiflora 'Loddon Anna'
Erigeron karvinskianus
Rosmarinus officinalis 'Capri'
Stachys byzantina

BIRD'S NEST

Trees & Shrubs
Elaeagnus ebbingei
Hippophae rhamnoides
Mahonia eurybracteata 'Soft Caress'
Pinus sylvestris
Quercus ilex
Rhus typhina
Tamarix tetrandra
Yucca gloriosa

Perennials & Grasses
Achillea 'Moonshine'
Carex testacea
Crocosmia 'Lucifer'
Echinacea purpurea 'Pica Bella'
Erigeron karvinskianus
Erysimum 'Bowles Mauve'
Eupatorium maculatum 'Atropurpureum'
Euphorbia characias 'Wulfenii'
Geranium 'Rozanne'
Origanum vulgare 'Compactum'
Stachys byzantina 'Silver Carpet'
Thymus vulgaris
Verbena bonariensis

ATELIERS VAN LISSUM

Trees & Shrubs
Carpinus betulus
Fatsia japonica
Hydrangea villosa
Platanus acerifolia

Climbers
Wisteria sinensis

Perennials & Grasses
Calamagrostis acutiflora 'Karl Foerster'
Euphorbia characias 'Wulfenii'

Miscanthus sinensis 'Malepartus'
Persicaria amplexicaulis 'Speciosa'

ATELIERS VAN LISSUM ROOF GARDEN

Trees & Shrubs
Amelanchier lamarckii
Carpinus betulus
Crataegus monogyna
Euphorbia characias 'Wulfenii'
Fagus sylvatica
Ligustrum vulgare
Osmanthus burkwoodii
Prunus spinosa
Rosa rugosa
Viburnum tinus

Perennials & Grasses
Aster amethystinus 'Freiburg'
Calamagrostis acutiflora 'Karl Foerster'
Carex testacea
Echinacea purpurea 'Pica Bella'
Erigeron karvinskianus
Eupatorium maculatum 'Atropurpureum'
Geranium 'Rozanne'
Helleborus orientalis
Miscanthus sinensis 'Malepartus'
Molinia caerulea 'Heidebraut'
Monarda 'Cambridge Scarlet'
Origanum vulgare
Persicaria amplexicaulis 'Speciosa'
Rosmarinus officinalis
Salvia nemorosa 'Ostfriesland'
Sedum 'Herbstfreude'
Thymus vulgaris
Verbena bonariensis

PANORAMA

Trees & Shrubs
Fatsia japonica
Nandina domestica
Prunus lusitanica 'Angustifolia'
Rhus typhina

Perennials & Grasses
Asplenium scolopendrium
Carex morrowii 'Mosten'
Galium odoratum
Helleborus orientalis

Liriope muscari
Muehlenbeckia axillaris
Ophiopogon planiscapus 'Niger'
Polystichum setiferum
Soleirolia soleirolii

PANTHEON

Trees & Shrubs
Catalpa bignonioides
Gleditsia triacanthos
Hydrangea macrophylla 'Twist-n-Shout'
Ilex aquifolium
Mahonia eurybracteata 'Soft Caress'

Climbers
Trachelospermum jasminoides

Perennials & Grasses
Acanthus mollis
Alcea rosea 'Nigra'
Anemone hybrida 'Honorine Jobert'
Brunnera macrophylla
Campanula portenschlagiana
Crocosmia 'Lucifer'
Erigeron karvinskianus
Erysimum 'Bowles Mauve'
Euphorbia characias 'Wulfenii'
Galium odoratum
Helleborus orientalis
Iris germanica 'Draco'
Kniphofia 'Papaya Popsicle'
Liriope muscari
Nepeta faassenii 'Walker's Low'
Stachys byzantina 'Silver Carpet'
Taxus baccata
Thymus vulgaris
Verbena bonariensis

RIVER SCHELDT

Trees & Shrubs
Amelanchier lamarckii
Ceanothus thyrsiflorus 'Repens'
Elaeagnus ebbingei
Rhus typhina
Rosa rugosa

Climbers
Wisteria sinensis

Perennials & Grasses
Campanula portenschlagiana

Carex howardii 'Phoenix Green'
Euphorbia characias 'Wulfenii'
Helleborus orientalis
Iris germanica 'Bianca'
Iris pseudacorus
Nepeta faassenii 'Purrsian Blue'
Stachys byzantina

FORGE

Trees & Shrubs
Ceanothus thyrsiflorus 'Repens'
Elaeagnus ebbingei
Hippophae rhamnoides
Pinus mugo 'Mugo'
Pinus vulgaris
Rhus typhina
Rosa rugosa
Tamarisk tetandra
Yucca gloriosa

Perennials & Grasses
Achillea 'Moonshine'
Centranthus ruber 'Coccineus'
Echinacea purpurea 'Pica Bella'
Eupatorium purpureum
Euphorbia characias 'Wulfenii'
Foeniculum vulgare 'Giant Bronze'
Iris germanica 'Black Knight'
Persicaria amplexicaulis 'JS Caliente'
Rosmarinus officinalis
Rudbeckia fulgida 'Goldsturm'
Verbena bonariensis

KLINGELBEEK ENTRY

Trees & Shrubs
Acer palmatum
Arbutus unedo
Edgeworthia chrysantha 'Grandiflora'
Fargesia robusta 'Campbell'
Fatsia japonica
Helleborus orientalis
Lagerstroemia indica
Mahonia media 'Charity'
Nandinia domestica
Tamarix tetrandra
Trachycarpus fortunei

Perennials & Grasses
Helleborus orientalis
Persicaria amplexicaulis 'Speciosa'

KLINGELBEEK PATIO

Trees & Shrubs
Acer palmatum
Camellia sasanqua
Eriobotrya japonica
Mahonia eurybracteata 'Soft Caress'
Osmanthus heterophyllus
Quercus ilex
Rhus typhina

Climbers
Wisteria sinensis

Perennials & Grasses
Campanula porscharskyana
Carex testacea
Euphorbia characias 'Wulfenii'
Geranium 'Ann Folkard'
Miscanthus sinensis 'Kleine Fontäne'
Persicaria amplexicaulis 'Speciosa'
Soleirolia soleirolii

KLINGELBEEK BEDROOM

Trees & Shrubs
Pinus sylvestris
Quercus ilex
Rhus typhina
Rosa rugosa
Tamarix ramosissima 'Pink Cascade'
Tamarix tetrandra
Yucca gloriosa

Perennials & Grasses
Erigeron karvinskianus
Euphorbia characias 'Wulfenii'
Euphorbia myrsinites
Geranium 'Rozanne'
Helleborus orientalis
Iris pumila 'Blue Denim'
Lavandula angustifolia 'Hidcote'
Rosmarinus officinalis
Santolina chamaecyparissus
Thymus vulgaris
Verbena bonariensis

Wild Harmony
Urban Gardens by Bart & Pieter

Pieter Croes
Bart Haverkamp

Photography
Anoek Luyten
Bart Kiggen (p 14-15, 90-95, 194-199, 217, 218-219)
Except for p 6-13, 208-211, 216 (private photos by Bart & Pieter et al.)

Editing
Hadewijch Ceulemans

Graphic Design
Bart Kiggen

Translation
Sandy Logan

D/2025/12.005/7
ISBN 9789460583810
NUR 425

2025 Luster Publishing, Antwerp
www.lusterpublishing.com
Printed in the Netherlands

Sign up for our newsletter for updates on new books and a behind-the-scenes look.

Special thanks to
Anoek Luyten and Bart Kiggen
Marc Verhagen, Dettie Luyten and Hadewijch at Luster Publishing
Bart Schoonderbeek and Rhüne, for encouraging us to create this book.

Our team and partners: Wouter Legrand, Rik Van Aert, Steven Nietvelt and Dries De Greef, Solitair tree nursery (solitair.be), Orangerie Jaeken (orangeriejaeken.be), Dockx&co (disaghordockx.be), Willaert Boomkwekerij (willaert.be) and Renaat De Neef (greenerycreations.be), and VIC Landschapes, for their support with the landscaping at IPKW and Klingelbeek.

The architects of the projects in this book: Machteld D'Hollander (Celine), Tine Bulckaen (Printery), Met Zicht op Zee (NH), Schipper Bosch / Space Encounters (IPKW), B-architecten (PSLab & Anyplace), Nathalie Wolberg (Paris / Texas), Filip Deslee (Loft 4C), TENARCHITECTS (PAC), Archipl Architecten (Burg), HUB (AMS), Elisa Perahia (Pantheon), Eva De Clerck (Dam), Dyvik Kahlen (Klingelbeek), Piet Pepermans (Ateliers Van Lissum).

All rights reserved. No part of this publication may be reproduced, stored in a retrieval system, or transmitted, in any form or by any means, without the prior written consent of the publisher. An exception is made for short excerpts, which may be cited for the sole purpose of reviews.